READING POWER

Famous American Trails

The Wilderness Road

From the Shenandoah Valley to the Ohio River

Arlan Dean

The Rosen Publishing Group's
PowerKids Press™
New York

Published in 2003 by The Rosen Publishing Group, Inc.
29 East 21st Street, New York, NY 10010

First Edition

Book Design: Christopher Logan

Photo Credits: Cover courtesy Washington University Gallery of Art, St. Louis, Missouri; pp. 4–5 © Hulton/Archive/Getty Images; p. 5 (inset) Christopher Logan; pp. 6–7, 13, 17 (inset) Library of Congress, Prints and Photographs Division; pp. 8, 9, 12, 16, 17, 18, 19, 21 © North Wind Picture Archives; pp. 10–11, 20 © AP/Wide World Photos; pp. 14–15 © Martin Fox/Index Stock Imagery, Inc.; back cover © Eyewire

Library of Congress Cataloging-in-Publication Data

Dean, Arlan.
The Wilderness Road : from the Shenandoah Valley to the Ohio River / Arlan Dean.
   p. cm. — (Famous American trails)
Summary: Introduces the two hundred mile Wilderness Road that began in Virginia and ended in Kentucky.
Includes bibliographical references and index.
ISBN 0-8239-6477-9 (lib. bdg.)
1. Wilderness Road—Juvenile literature. 2. Frontier and pioneer life—Kentucky—Juvenile literature. 3. Frontier and pioneer life—Tennessee—Juvenile literature. 4. Frontier and pioneer life—Virginia—Juvenile literature. 5. Boone, Daniel, 1734-1820—Juvenile literature. 6. Kentucky—Description and travel—Juvenile literature. 7. Tennessee—Description and travel—Juvenile literature. 8. Virginia—Description and travel—Juvenile literature. [1. Wilderness Road. 2. Frontier and pioneer life. 3. Boone, Daniel, 1734-1820.] I. Title.
F454 .D43 2003
976.8—dc21
                                                    2002002939

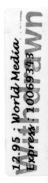

Contents

Going West   4

Daniel Boone Makes a Trail   8

Boonesborough   12

Using the Wilderness Road   14

End of the Trail   20

Glossary   22

Resources   23

Index/Word Count   24

Note   24

Going West

Most early settlers in America lived along the east coast. Their settlements were usually less than 100 miles from the Atlantic Ocean. By the late 1700s, many people wanted to move west to find new places to live and work. One of the paths these pioneers used to travel west was called the Wilderness Road.

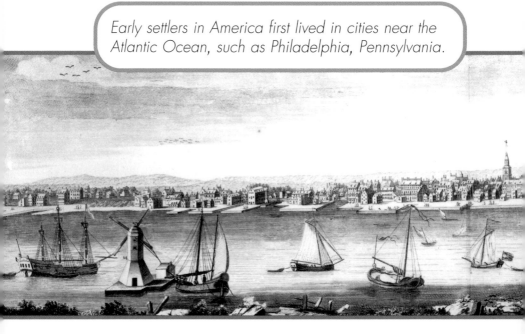

Early settlers in America first lived in cities near the Atlantic Ocean, such as Philadelphia, Pennsylvania.

THE WILDERNESS ROAD

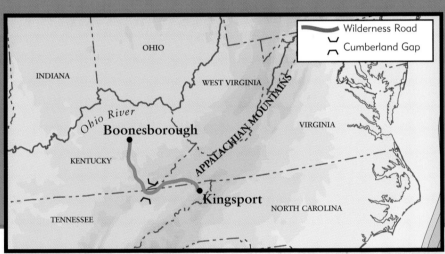

Settlers moving west had to cross the Appalachian Mountains. In 1750, Dr. Thomas Walker was one of the first explorers to reach the Cumberland Gap, a natural pass through the mountains. He mapped the area and gave the gap its name.

The Cumberland Gap is near the point where the states of Tennessee, Virginia, and Kentucky meet.

Daniel Boone Makes a Trail

American pioneer and explorer Daniel Boone made a trip to Kentucky through the Cumberland Gap in 1769. Boone saw that the land in Kentucky was good for farming and hunting.

Check It Out

June 7 is Boone Day in the state of Kentucky. Daniel Boone first saw Kentucky on this date in 1769.

In 1775, Richard Henderson, a businessman, hired Boone to make a trail west to Kentucky. Boone hired 30 men to help him clear a path.

Daniel Boone

Boone and his group connected Native American trails and animal trails to make the passage to the West. Boone also used the Cumberland Gap as part of the new trail. He and his men used axes to cut down bushes and trees to clear the path.

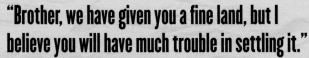

"Brother, we have given you a fine land, but I believe you will have much trouble in settling it."
—A Native American, speaking to Daniel Boone after signing a treaty agreeing to turn over Kentucky to settlers

Boone cut a mark on a large tree at the end of each mile of trail that was cleared.

Boonesborough

When Daniel Boone and his men arrived in Kentucky, they started a settlement called Boonesborough.

The Boonesborough fort was built near the Kentucky River, just south of present-day Lexington, Kentucky.

They built cabins and planted crops. Boone also had the men build a fort to protect the new settlement.

Boone's cabin in Kentucky

Using the Wilderness Road

Boone's trail soon became known as the Wilderness Road. At that time, it was the only usable trail through the Appalachian Mountains to Kentucky. After Boonesborough was built, many settlers used the trail to travel west.

The Appalachian Mountains run from southeastern Canada to the state of Alabama, in the United States. Smaller mountain ranges, such as the Catskill Mountains, the Green Mountains, and the Great Smoky Mountains make up the Appalachian Mountains.

Check It Out

By 1800, about 200,000 settlers had passed through the Cumberland Gap and traveled along the Wilderness Road to Kentucky.

The trip along the Wilderness Road was very hard. The trail was bumpy and narrow. At first, the Wilderness Road was only wide enough for horses to use.

Before the Wilderness Road was made wider, only horses could pass through the narrow trails.

In 1796, the road was made wider so wagons could use it, too. After the road was widened, people from Kentucky used it to bring horses and cattle to markets in the East.

Check It Out

Among the people who traveled the Wilderness Road to Kentucky were Ulysses S. Grant, George Rogers Clark, and Abraham Lincoln's mother Nancy Hanks.

Ulysses S. Grant

Wagons on the Wilderness Road

Travelers on the Wilderness Road were often attacked by Native Americans. The Native Americans were angry because the settlers were taking their hunting lands.

Native Americans often tried to drive settlers out of Kentucky.

Native Americans used the land in Kentucky as their hunting grounds.

End of the Trail

By the 1840s, the Wilderness Road was not often used. People had made new trails for traveling west. Today, there is a national park at Cumberland Gap.

The Wilderness Road made it possible for thousands of people to travel west so they could find a better way of life. It played an important part in the growth of America.

Today, there are many markers along the Wilderness Road that honor the early travelers who used it.

Part of the Wilderness Road can be seen at the Levi Jackson Wilderness Road State Park in Kentucky.

The Wilderness Road Time Line

1750	Dr. Thomas Walker reaches the Cumberland Gap.
1769	Daniel Boone crosses into Kentucky through the Cumberland Gap.
1775	Boone marks the trail that will become the Wilderness Road.
1796	The Wilderness Road is widened so wagons can use it.
1840s	People stop using the Wilderness Road to go west.

Glossary

explorer (ehk-**splor**-uhr) a person who searches
for new places

fort (**fort**) a strong building or place that can
easily be guarded

national (**nash**-uh-nuhl) belonging to the government

passage (**pas**-ihj) an opening or a path
for getting from one place to another

pioneer (py-uh-**nihr**) someone who goes first
to prepare a way for others

settlement (**seht**-l-muhnt) a place where people
come to live

settlers (**seht**-luhrz) people who come to stay
in a new country or place

treaty (**tree**-tee) an official understanding,
signed and agreed upon by two or more nations

wilderness (**wihl**-duhr-nihs) a place that has not
been touched by people and where people
have never lived

Resources

Books

*Daniel Boone and the Opening
of the Ohio Country*
by Seamus Cavan
Chelsea House Publishers (1991)

Daniel Boone and the Wilderness Road
by Catherine E. Chambers
Troll Communications (1998)

Web Sites

Due to the changing nature of Internet links, PowerKids
Press has developed an online list of Web sites related
to the subjects of this book. This site is updated regularly.
Please use this link to access the list:

http://www.powerkidslinks.com/fat/wilr/

Index

A

Appalachian
    Mountains, 5–6, 14

B

Boone, Daniel,
    8–14, 21

C

Cumberland Gap,
    5–6, 8, 10, 15,
    20–21

E

explorer, 6, 8

F

fort, 12–13

N

Native American, 11,
    18–19

P

passage, 10
pioneer, 4, 8

S

settlement, 4, 12–13
settlers, 4, 6, 11,
    14–15, 18

T

trail, 9–11, 14,
    16, 21

Word Count: 500

Note to Librarians, Teachers, and Parents

    If reading is a challenge, Reading Power is a solution! Reading Power
is perfect for readers who want high-interest subject matter at an accessible reading
level. These fact-filled, photo-illustrated books are designed for readers who want
straightforward vocabulary, engaging topics, and a manageable reading experience.
With clear picture/text correspondence, leveled Reading Power books put the reader
in charge. Now readers have the power to get the information they want and the skills
they need in a user-friendly format.